Little Pigs, Big Pigs

Learning the Short I Sound

Shelby Braidich

Phonics for the REAL World™

Rosen Classroom Books and Materials™
New York

Pigs are farm animals.

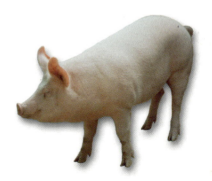

Some pigs are little.

Some pigs are big.

Pigs live in yards.

Pigs sleep in pens.

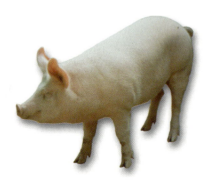

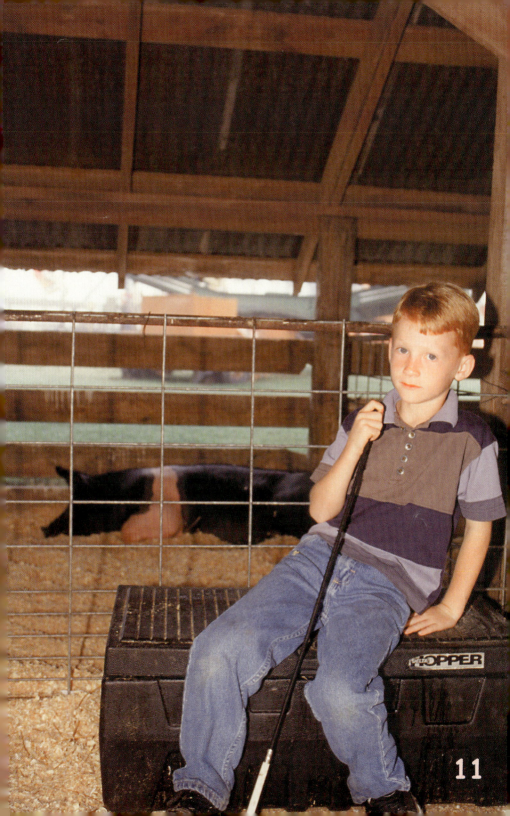

Pigs play in mud.

Pigs have four feet.

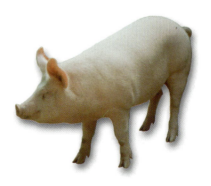

Pigs have tails.

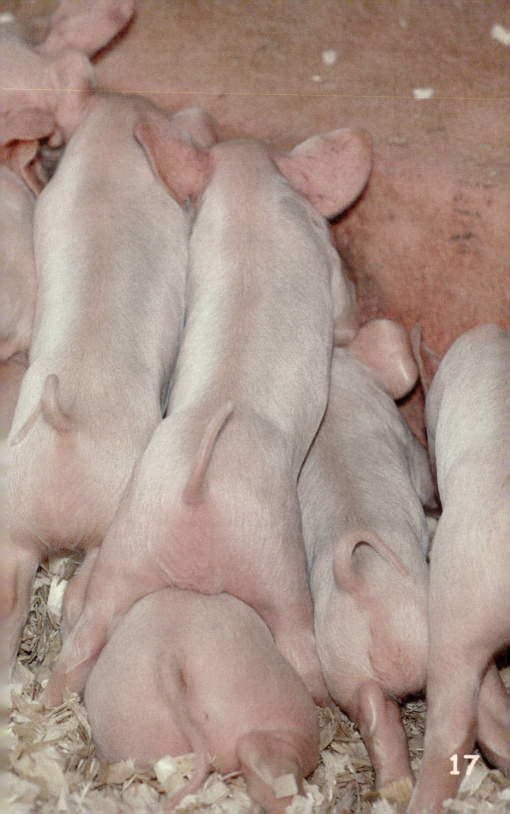

Some pigs are pink.

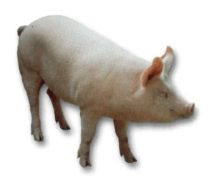

Kids like pigs!

Word List

big

in

kids

little

live

pigs

pink

Instructional Guide

Note to Instructors:
One of the essential skills that enable a young child to read is the ability to associate letter-sound symbols and blend these sounds to form words. Phonics instruction can teach children a system that will help them decode unfamiliar words and, in turn, enhance their word-recognition skills. We offer a phonics-based series of books that are easy to read and understand. Each book pairs words and pictures that reinforce specific phonetic sounds in a logical sequence. Topics are based on curriculum goals appropriate for early readers in the areas of science, social studies, and health.

Letter/Sound: **short i** – List the following words: *kick, kids, kindergarten, king, kitchen, kitten*. Ask: "What letter do all these words begin with?" Have the child underline the initial **k** in all the words. Ask: "How else are all these words alike?" Have the child underline the **short i** in each word.
- Pronounce the following pair of words: *big – bag*. Have the child name the one that, like the initial **k** words above, has the **short i** vowel sound. Continue with other pairs of words: *fat – fit, dig – dog, ham – him, sit – sat,* etc. List the child's responses. Add other familiar **short i** words to the list. Have the child use the words in sentences. Have the child underline the **short i** in each word.

Phonics Activities: On a chalkboard or dry-erase board, write incomplete words, such as: *b__t, t__n, s__p,* etc. Have the child complete the words by writing the missing **short i**. Ask them to decode the completed words and use them in sentences.
- Provide the child with *yes* and *no* response cards. Have them hold up the correct card in response to the following: "Will you ever see a pig in a wig?" (Continue with: *a pig that is big, a pig dancing a jig, a pig eating a fig.* Follow with: *a pig that is pink, a pig taking a drink, a pig that can think.*) List the rhyming words and have the child underline the **short i** in each of them.
- Write the following word endings on the board: *ib, it, ig, ip, ill, in.* Have the child see how many words they can make for each word family. (Examples: *bib, crib, rib, kit, lit, sit, fit, big, wig, dig, tip, lip, sip, nip, bill, will, dill, chill, fin, pin, sin, win.*) Have the child practice reading the new words.

Additional Resources:
- Doudna, Kelly. *Piglets*. Minneapolis, MN: ABDO Publishing Company, 2000.
- Gibbons, Gail. *Pigs*. New York: Holiday House, Inc., 1999.
- Miller, Sara S. *Pigs*. Danbury, CT: Children's Press, 2000.

Published in 2002 by The Rosen Publishing Group, Inc.
29 East 21st Street, New York, NY 10010

Copyright © 2002 by The Rosen Publishing Group, Inc.

All rights reserved. No part of this book may be reproduced in any form without permission in writing from the publisher, except by a reviewer.

Book Design: Ron A. Churley

Photo Credits: Cover, p. 3 © Kirk Anderson/Animals Animals; p. 5 © Leonard L. T. Rhodes/Animals Animals; p. 7 © SuperStock; p. 9 © Wendy Neefus/Animals Animals; p. 11 © Allen Russell/Index Stock; pp. 13, 21 © Lynn Stone/Animals Animals; p. 15 © Fritz Prenzel/Animals Animals; p. 17 © Sydney Thomson/Animals Animals; p. 19 © Scott Smith/Animals Animals.

Library of Congress Cataloging-in-Publication Data

Braidich, Shelby, 1971-
 Little pigs, big pigs : learning the short I sound / author, Shelby Braidich.
   p. cm. — (Power phonics/phonics for the real world)
 ISBN 0-8239-5904-X (library binding)
 ISBN 0-8239-8249-1 (pbk.)
 6 pack ISBN 0-8239-9217-9
 1. Swine—Juvenile literature. 2. English language—Vowels—Juvenile literature. [1. Pigs. 2. English language—Vowels.] I. Title. II. Series.
SF395.5 .B74 2002
636.4—dc21
                                            2001000588

Manufactured in the United States of America